DANIEL    Four friends are taken to Babylon (ch. 1)

DANIEL     A diet of vegetables and water (ch. 1)

DANIEL     Nebuchadnezzar asks about his dream (ch. 2)     © 1998 GO TEACH PUBLICATIONS LTD

DANIEL       Daniel tells the king his dream (ch. 2)

DANIEL          Shadrach, Meshach and Abednego refuse to bow (ch. 3)          © 1998 GO TEACH PUBLICATIONS LTD

DANIEL

DANIEL    A fourth figure appears in the furnace (ch. 3)    © 1998 GO TEACH PUBLICATIONS LTD

MENE, ME

DANIEL    King Belshazzar sees a hand writing (ch. 5)    © 1998 GO TEACH PUBLICATIONS LTD

MENE, ME...
TEKEL,
PARSI...

DANIEL    Daniel explains the writing on the wall (ch. 5)    © 1998 GO TEACH PUBLICATIONS LTD

DANIEL      King Darius makes a law forbidding prayer (ch. 6)      © 1998 GO TEACH PUBLICATIONS LTD

DANIEL    Daniel in the lions' den (ch. 6)